Recipes of Motivation

By: Chef Marvin Jones

Copyright © 2023 by Marvin Jones

All rights reserved

Published by:

Writers of the West (www.writersofthewest.net)

All rights reserved. No part of this publication may be reproduced, distributed, or transmitted in any form or by any means, including photocopying, recording, or other electronic or mechanical methods, without the prior written permission of the author.

Trademarks: This book identifies product names, dishes & services known to be trademarks or service marks of their respective holders. The author acknowledges the trademarked status and trademark owners of all products and places referenced in this work of fiction. The publication and use of these trademarks is not authorized, associated with, or sponsored by the trademark owners.

New Castle, Delaware

Printed in the United States of America

First Printing – November 2023

Intro

Recipes of Motivation is the first book of a 3 book trilogy series.

This book is a creatively written monologue of positive paragraphs and recipes to motivate and inspire the hands of meal preparation.

"Live Your Life Larger Than the Portions on Your Plate"

This book, written from a chef's point of view to inspire you to find the purpose of your "Why," develop your "God-given potential," and to pursue your dreams to the fullest.

<u>On The Cutting Edge.</u>

A hard-hitting, eat-or-be-eaten, beyond-the-scope-of-the-stratosphere motivational read. My perspective in written this book is to encourage us, as human beings, to return to our true place as the highest order of creation on Planet Earth.

Dedication

This book is dedicated to my mother.

Mom, I know that when you passed away on October 10, 2010, the gates of heaven were wide open when you entered.

And without you, I wouldn't be the man I am today. Please continue to watch over me, and I will strive to make you proud for as long as I live.

Acknowledgements

To my GOD – I'm truly blessed to be a part of your great creation. I'm forever grateful for all that I have and for all that you continue to do for me. Let them see you through the miracle you have for me! To my daughter and my grandchildren, you're all that I have and I love you dearly! To my sister "it's me and you, Sis."

Chef M's

Seven Signature Suppers

- Chicken Marvicasso
- Turkey Shepherd's Pie
- Three Meat Lasagna
- Baked Salmon, Shrimp & Lobster Newburg
- Vegan Chili with Whole Grain Cornbread
- Flank Steak with Mushrooms, Red Bliss Potatoes & Asparagus
- Slice Pork loin with Peach Sauce

Soup & Salad Supper

- ChefM Signature Salad
- Cream of Jalapeno Pepper & Black Bean Soup

CM's Dessert Creations

- Gemini Cake

Special Message from Chef Marvin Jones

Life itself is an inspirational miracle, and I have been inspired by all things during the course of my journey in the gift of living this daily miracle.

I see and take in the visionary process to create my thoughts of inspiration. I don't believe that we find or define ourselves during the living process of life. I believe that we "create" ourselves.

Remember, GOD "created" all things and life, and we survive every single day of living it. So, this revolutionary process of survival is the reason why we exist today.

"GOD, let them see You in all that I do"

Table Of Contents

Intro *4*
Dedication *6*
Acknowledgements *7*
Chef Marvin's Specials: *8*
Special Message from Chef Marvin Jones *9*
1 Your Ingredients for Success *12*
    ChefM Salad *13*
2 Getting Your Kitchen in Order *16*
    The First Meal of the Day: *17*
    Three Cheese Omelet *17*
3 Slices of Pie *20*
    Time for a Slice of Pie *21*
    Sweet Potato-Apple Pie with Walnut Crumb Topping *21*
4 Creating Your Dish *24*
    The Creation of Chicken Marvicasso *25*
5 Be Always Hungry *27*
    Desire Hunger *28*
    A Hungry Man's Dinner *28*
    Grilled Flank Steak with Mushrooms: *29*
    Mashed Cauliflower & Red Potatoes: *31*
    Green Bean & Corn Medley: *32*
    Sweet Potato Biscuits with Herb Butter: *33*
    Herb Butter *35*

6 More Salt & Pepper, Please *36*
   Two Spice Up *37*
   Black Bean and Cream of Jalapeno Soup *37*
   Black Bean Soup: *37*
   Cream of Jalapeno Soup: *39*

7 Sweet or Sour Palate *41*
   Talk is Sweet *42*
   Sweet & Sour Salmon *42*

8 Thanksgiving is Every Meal *45*
   A Meal to be Thankful For *46*
   Turkey Shepherd's Pie *46*

9 The Journey of Seasons & Spices *50*
   Drink Up *51*
   The 8th Wonder of the World Drink *51*

10 The Melting Pot *53*
   Diversity Stew *54*
   Harty Vegetable Vegan Stew *54*

11 Time to Serve *57*
   Cooking Times of Service *58*

12 Beyond the Two Layer Cake *62*
   Your Cake Layers *63*
   Gemini Brownie Marble Cake *63*

About the Author *70*

1

Your Ingredients for

Success

Mindset is everything, and everything else follows. Your perspective on how you view the world develops from the early beginnings of your life, shaped through your exposures, experiences, evaluations of things learned, social relationships, core values, and the crucial decision of never-ending choices to be made. If you encompass all that has stimulated your senses as a human being, it makes up who you truly are and is the essence of what you are made of. To "make" is to incorporate parts of useful things to form the creation of something that is complete.

Using a culinary comparison, the preparation of making a salad comes to mind. There are five ingredients used as the basis of making a salad; the Greens, Vegetables, Fruit, a Protein source, and a type of Dressing. Similarly, in the context of the five senses of a human being – Sight, Hearing, Touch, Taste and Smell – the preparing process of making the Salad is a metaphor for the development of oneself. The ingredients used in the development of self are crucial in creating your life's success.

ChefM Salad

Just because it's called the ChefM Salad doesn't mean that everyone else can't make their own version. Whether you're a chef or not, you can use other ingredients to create an exclusive version!

- Vegan ChefM Salad
- Pescatarian ChefM Salad
- The Classic ChefM Salad

Ingredients:

- 1 head each of iceberg, romaine & green leaf lettuce, cored and hand-pulled into bite-size pieces
- 1 small onion, sliced

- 3 hard-boiled eggs, cut into wedges
- 1 small cucumber, sliced
- ¼ pound thinly sliced cheddar cheese
- 2 cups of black olives, cut in half
- ½ pound sliced turkey, cut into strips
- 2 medium-sized tomatoes, wedge cut
- ½ pound sliced ham, cut into strips
- 1 large green bell pepper, flower cut
- ½ cup of crumbled walnuts

Yield: 4 portions

Instructions:

1. Place the prepared three lettuce combo (iceberg, romaine, and green leaf lettuce), along with the onion, cucumber, and black olives in a large serving bowl. Toss lightly and arrange the flower cut green bell peppers on top.
2. Arrange the turkey, ham and cheese in rows over the lettuce. Top with tomatoes, eggs and crumbled walnuts.
3. Serve with Creamy Italian Dressing or any other dressings of your choice.

2

Getting Your Kitchen in Order

Preparation and being organized are key elements that will assuredly fit into your planning program. The process of achieving your end goals is a victory, and the journey toward realizing your perception can be considerably less of a battle if your plan of attack is well-strategized. In very simple terms, it's all about taking the time to plan, think things through, and set yourself up for success.

Whatever it is in life that you are called to do or desire to accomplish:

1. **Visualize it:** If you see that dream in your mind than you can hold it in your hands.
2. **Journalize it:** Write down your thoughts and goals daily.

3. **Plan It:** Decide your approach, arrange things in advance and follow through.

   The military approach, which I am accustomed to from my time in the United States Marines Corps, involved an apparent memory. When we were presented with a planned mission, we didn't stop until that mission was completed. Moreover, in memory of my service in the military was that with all of the planned training that we had to accomplish during the course of a day, breakfast was truly the most important meal.

The First Meal of the Day: Three Cheese Omelet

There should be order in everything that you do, and the same applies to the preparation of making an omelet. So, to keep it basic for the first meal of the day, here are the steps for preparing a three-cheese chef's omelet.

Other Omelet Styles: Explore various omelet styles other than the classic three-cheese omelet:

➢ French Omelet

- Rolled Omelet
- Flat/Dollar Bill Omelet

Instructions:

1. Whisks 2 to 3 eggs in small bowl, and add salt and pepper if desired. If preparing a **French Omelet** add milk or cream.
2. Heat butter or olive oil in a 7-inch non-stick pan.
3. Add the seasoned egg mixture to the heated pan.
4. As the eggs cook, gently lift up the edges so that the mixture can cook evenly.
5. Flip the entire omelet to cook the other side in the pan.
6. Add your choice of three cheeses.
7. Fold the cooked omelet in half and serve. Garnish with parsley or sliced scallions if desired!

Note: If you wish to add other ingredients to your omelet such as; ham, sausage, mushrooms, spinach, or tomatoes, sauté these ingredients during step 2 before adding the egg mixture.

3

Slices of Pie

Time is an indispensable commodity. There is no price tag that can be placed on it because once it's gone, it's gone. Time is the fairest present bestowed upon mankind. Everyone regardless of their background receives 24 hours of time every day on planet Earth. We've all heard the expression, "Use Your Time Wisely". Let's draw an analogy to **"Slices of Pie".** You have the choice of how big or small a slice from your time-pie you want to use during the course of any given day. Let's put it another way, you decide whether you want to spend a significant part of your time on activities like watching television, using social media, or playing video games, etc., versus dedicating time to more productive things such as working out, reading educational books, or learn new skills to better yourself. The portions of your time slices are all in your hands. Effective time management enables you to work on your goals, make substantial progress in achieving balance and control, and assign time to do the things that truly matter in your life.

Time for a Slice of Pie Sweet Potato-Apple Pie with Walnut Crumb Topping

Everybody desires their slice of the pie, and there's no better way to start than by baking the whole pie. This pie will satisfy both apple pie and sweet potato enthusiasts, offering a mouth-watering amalgam of flavors. Here is what you'll need to get your slice:

Ingredients for the Pie Filling:

- 4 medium Granny Smith Apples (approx. 2 pounds)
- 3 medium Sweet Potatoes (approx. 2 pounds)
- ¼ cup of Tapioca Starch
- 1 cup of Brown Sugar
- 1 1/2 teaspoons of Ground Cinnamon
- 1 teaspoon of Nutmeg
- ¼ cup of Pure Vanilla Extract

- 1 Deep Dish Pie Shell or Homemade Pie Dough (follow the instructions)
- 1 tablespoon of freshly squeezed Lemon Juice

Ingredients for the Crumb Topping:

- 1 cup of Pecans, Crumbled
- ¾ cup of All-Purpose Flour
- ½ cup of Granulated Sugar
- ¼ cup of Brown Sugar
- 1 tablespoon of Ground Cinnamon
- ½ teaspoon of All-Spice
- 1 ½ cups of unsalted melted Butter

Instructions:

1. Peel, core, and slice apples lengthwise into 1/2-inch-thick wedges. Place the apple slices in a mixing bowl with lemon juice, mix thoroughly, and set aside. Meanwhile, peel and quarter sweet potatoes lengthwise, and slice them into 1/2-inch wedges. Bring water in a 3-quart saucepan to a boil and cook sweet potatoes until they are tender. Drain the sweet potatoes and rinse them under cold water. Set them aside to let cool to room temperature.

2. After about 15 minutes, allowing the apples to macerate, add the sweet potatoes, tapioca starch, brown sugar, cinnamon, nutmeg and vanilla extract. Toss to combine. Pour sweet potatoes and apples, along with accumulated syrup, into the prepared pie shell.
3. Preheat the oven to 350 degrees. Meanwhile, in a medium heatproof bowl, combine all-purpose flour, granulated sugar, brown sugar, cinnamon, and all-spice. In a blender, pulse pecans until roughly chopped, about 5 seconds. Add them to the flour mixture. Pour melted butter over the flour mixture. Using a rubber spatula, thoroughly mix until no dry flour remains, adding more butter if needed.
4. Evenly distribute the crumble topping over pie filling, breaking up any large chunks with your fingers. Place the pie on a parchment-lined sheet pan and bake it in the center of the oven for about 45 minutes. If the crumble topping starts to darken, loosely cover the pie with aluminum foil for the remainder of the baking time.
5. Transfer the pie to a wire rack and let it cool to room temperature for about 1 hour. Slice and serve.

   Enjoy the slice of this delicious Sweet Potato-Apple Pie!

4

Creating Your Dish

Life isn't about finding yourself but about creating yourself. Personal development and self-improvement are the driving forces that lead you toward a successful life. The more you learn and apply in your personal growth as a human being, the more you create "Experiences of Value" that become useful on your life's journey. Creating the individual, you aspire to become starts with a positive perspective about improving upon your present self. My exposure and schooling in the development process over 30 years of becoming the Chef that I am today, has been vital. With that "Exposure of Experience," when I'm preparing and experimenting with ingredients, seasoning, spices, or sauces to create a new dish, I can literally visualize how the end product will turn out. The visualization is the result of years of applied experiences to my craft of cooking. Even while attending Culinary School, I preferred to experiment and create my own version than follow the lead. I always enjoy my version of the entrée.

Creativity is the skill of using imagination to bring new things to life, which is why I created a dish named after myself...

The Creation of Chicken Marvicasso

One of the main reasons I developed a great passion for cooking is the fact that it combines technical skills with artistry. Creating a dish is much like composing a piece of art, with the goal of achieving balance in textures, visual appeal, flavor, and colors. However, unlike artwork displayed on a canvas, the dish being created is meant to be enjoyed and savored! Many of the great artist of the past didn't share the painting techniques, many present-day chefs also won't reveal their recipe trade secrets or signature dishes. While I can't disclose the entire recipe for my signature dish **"Chicken Marvicasso,"** I can only share the list of ingredients:

Ingredients:

- Fresh Boneless Chicken Breast
- Wild Rice
- Mushrooms
- Green Tomatoes
- Black Olives
- Red Bell Pepper
- Onions
- Shallots
- Capers
- ChefM's Marvicasso Sauce

I hope to assemble this signature dish for you in its entirety one day.

5

Be Always Hungry

The hunger of a lion feeds its desire to stay motivated and persistent in order to satisfy that hunger. Being hungry and being motivated for the purpose of making the point in this chapter are one and the same; if these two words were twins, then they would share the same desires. And that same desire should be of equal motivation and persistence in the pursuit of your dreams or whatever it is that you are distant to do in life.

To be clear: When you find your God-given purpose, you are to spend every single day of your natural life being hungry in pursuit of that purpose. To live this life and die without knowing what you are meant to do is more tragic than dying. To live with purpose is to wake up every morning with creative meaning, to guide your life's decisions, influence behavior, be optimistic, have a sense of direction, shape and have a vision of your goals, and to lie down at night with a day full of fulfillment! Always feed your hunger for fulfillment in the never-ending "Pursuit of Purpose" by staying focused on the hunt to feed it, a mindset motivated to climb mountains for it, and destiny-driven determination to succeed at it. The plate of your success should never be empty, so always be hungry and feast on success.

Desire Hunger

A Hungry Man's Dinner

- ➢ Grilled Flank Steak with Mushrooms
- ➢ Mashed Cauliflower & Red Potatoes
- ➢ Green Bean and Corn Medley
- ➢ Sweet Potato Biscuits with Herb Butter

Not only is this meal hearty enough to satisfy anyone's appetite, it is also eye-catching!

Grilled Flank Steak with Mushrooms:

Ingredients:

- 1 Flank Steak, about 2 pounds
- 2 cups of Mushrooms, cut into quarters
- 1 cup of Worcestershire Sauce
- 2 tablespoons of Montreal Steak Seasoning
- ¼ cup of lemon juice (one lemon)
- 4 cloves minced Garlic
- 1 tablespoon of fresh Rosemary, chopped
- 2 tablespoons of Butter
- ¼ cup of Olive Oil
- 1 cup of Beef Broth
- 2 tablespoons of Cornstarch

Yield: 4 portions

Instructions:

1. Rub the flank steak with olive oil and marinate with Worcestershire sauce, lemon juice, Montreal Steak Seasoning, minced garlic for about an hour.
2. Grill the flank steak over high heat for about 7 minutes per side or until medium cooked. Let it rest for 10 minutes before slicing.
3. Add butter and the remaining olive oil to a saucepan and heat. Add rosemary and mushrooms and sauté for about 2 minutes.
4. Combine beef broth with cornstarch to make a slurry, then add it to the sauce pan. Cook until slightly thickened.
5. Slice the meat against the grain and serve with the mushrooms sauce.

Mashed Cauliflower & Red Potatoes:

Ingredients:

- 6 medium Red Potatoes, cut into quarters
- 1 small Cauliflower head, cored and cut into small pieces
- 2 tablespoons Butter
- Salt & Pepper

Instructions:

1. In a large pot, fill with 1/3 water, add salt, and bring to a boil, then add the cut red potatoes and cook for about 10 minutes.
2. Add the cut cauliflower to the same pot and cook for an additional 10 minutes or until the potatoes and cauliflower are fork-tender.
3. Drain and place back into the pot. Add butter, salt & pepper to taste.
4. Mash mixture with a potato masher until smooth to be served with entrée.

Green Bean & Corn Medley:

Ingredients:

- 3 cups of fresh Green Beans
- 2 cups of fresh-cut Corn
- 2 tablespoons of Butter
- 1 tablespoon of Olive Oil
- 1 tablespoon of dried Thyme leaves
- 1 teaspoon of Seasoning Salt

Instructions:

1. In a large skillet on low heat, sauté green beans and corn in butter and olive oil until tender. Stir in the thyme leaves and seasoning salt. Ready to be served with the entrée.

Sweet Potato Biscuits with Herb Butter:

Ingredients:

- 2 cups of cooked, mashed Sweet Potatoes (about 2 large sweet potatoes)
- 2 ¾ cups of all-purpose flour
- 1 tablespoon of Baking Powder
- 1 tablespoon of Brown Sugar
- 2 teaspoons of kosher salt
- ½ cup (1 stick) Butter, cold and cut into small cubes
- ½ cup of Heavy Cream
- Cold Melted butter for brushing

Instructions:

1. Preheat the oven to 350 degrees. In a large bowl, combine flour, baking powder, sugar, and salt. Add the small cuts of butter into the flour, mix with hands until about pea size.

2. Add mashed sweet potatoes and heavy cream and stir until a rough dough starts to form. Again, use hands to help knead flour until it incorporates together.
3. Place dough on a clean dusted flour surface. Form dough into a ½-inch-thick square, then fold the dough in half from left to right and again from top to bottom. With a rolling pin, roll out dough into a ¾-thick-square.
4. Use a 2 ½-inch round cutter to cut biscuits cut and place on a greased baking sheet. Gather the dough scraps together and pat back down into a ¾-inch-thick square one more time to cut a few more biscuits out.
5. Brush the tops of the biscuits with melted butter and bake in the preheated oven for approximately 20 minutes or until golden brown. Serve with the entrée.

Herb Butter

Ingredients:

- 4 tablespoons unsalted Butter, softened
- 1 tablespoon of Chives, chopped
- 3 Basil leaves, chopped
- 1 Parsley sprig, chopped

Instructions:

1. Mix together the butter and herbs. Serve with biscuits at room temperature.

6

More Salt & Pepper, Please

When a recipe calls for you to add a particular seasoning or spice for taste, it means that you can add as much of that ingredient as needed to enhance the flavor of the dish being prepared. Salt is a seasoning, pepper is a spice, and both are used in correlation to enhance the flavor of what is being prepared. As you prepare yourself for the journey of high-level betterment, enhancement as it relates to human potential has a host of ingredients in the improvement of the quality and value of oneself. Some ingredients that can be used or just wanting to add **"More Salt & Pepper"** to the recipe of self-improvement are: focus on your strengths for mental, physical, and spiritual growth, raise the value and advance to next level for personal gain, and increase the intensity of forward motion as not to stay stagnant. The preparation is endless in "spicing up" the human factor of performance in reaching your goals in life. So, if your "forward movement progress" seems to be "tasteless" or needs a little flavor enhancement. Add More Salt & Pepper, please!

Two Spice Up Black Bean and Cream of Jalapeno Soup

This is one of my signature soups and should be considered a famous combo staple like "Salt & Pepper" or "Peanut Butter & Jelly," and after preparing the recipe and tasting it…You'll see why!

Black Bean Soup:

Ingredients:

- 4 cans (15 ounces each) Black Beans, rinsed and drained
- 4 cups Vegetable Broth, low-sodium
- 2 medium Onions, finely chopped

- 3 Celery ribs, finely chopped
- 1 large Carrot, peeled and finely chopped
- 6 Garlic Cloves, minced
- 4 teaspoons of Ground Cumin
- Salt and fresh ground Pepper to taste
- 2 tablespoons of extra-virgin Olive Oil

Instructions:

1. In a large stock pot, heat the olive oil over medium heat, add the onions, celery, carrots, and garlic. Cook, stirring occasionally, until the vegetables are soft.
2. Pour in the black beans and vegetable broth, then add cumin, salt, and pepper to taste. Bring to a simmer, until the broth is flavorful and the beans are very tender, about 20 minutes.
3. Use an immersion blender to blend a portion of the soup until it slightly thickens. Keep warm until ready to serve with Cream of Jalapeno Soup.

Cream of Jalapeno Soup:

Ingredients:

- 5 fresh Jalapenos, stemmed, seeded and minced
- ¾ cup of finely chopped Onions
- 3 Garlic cloves, minced
- 6 cups of Milk
- 1 cup of Heavy Cream
- 1 stick of unsalted Butter
- ¼ cup of Flour
- Salt & freshly ground Black Pepper

Instructions:

1. In a large saucepan, heat the butter over medium heat. Add the jalapenos, onion, and garlic and sauté, stirring until the vegetables are softened, being sure not to brown. Remove the pan from the heat.
2. Add the flour to the saucepan, stirring with the butter and vegetables to incorporate a roux (flour & butter).
3. Lower the temperature and return the pan to heat, add milk and heavy cream, watching and stirring bring the soup

slowly to a simmer and cook. Be sure stir occasionally to prevent scorching.

4. Cook slowly for about 20 minutes or until the soup thickens (adjust desired thickness by adding more roux while cooking). Remove from heat at this time. Use a handheld immersion blender to slightly blend. Season with salt and pepper. Keep warm until ready to serve with Black Bean Soup.

Serving Instructions:

Separately but at the same time, ladle both the Black Bean and the Cream of Jalapeno into a soup bowl. These two soups should remain side-by-side in the bowl. Garnish with Tabasco sauce, crumbled tortilla chips, & lime. (optional)

*Portions are determined by bowl sizes being used.

7

Sweet or Sour Palate

Speech relies on the activation of multiple areas of the brain working together cooperatively. That, within itself, sounds pretty important! As I stated in chapter one; "Mindset is everything and everything else follows." And after thought, the words that are spoken out of your mouths usually comes next. So, for the purpose of this chapter, we are going to recognize the thought process of positive and negative self-talk, which can influence your actual conversational speech and circumstances. Generally, when you engage in positive (sweet) talk, you cope better with emotions and mental stress, improve confidence, self-esteem, and become more optimistic about life and your overall quality of life. While those who find themselves frequently engaging in negative (sour) talk tend to be more stressed, quick to label things as bad, find fault with everything, and are pessimistic. Staying mindful of "speaking into existence" your internal thoughts is ever so powerful! Putting your potential in the balance. It channels your desires and intentions out there into the universe, and the universe will conspire to make it happen...

Talk is Sweet

Sweet & Sour Salmon

This Sweet & Sour Salmon recipe is perfect for a super easy dinner that feeds two, which takes only 30 minutes to make, requires 10 ingredients, and is sure to tantalize your palate!

Ingredients:

- 2 Salmon filets with the skin on are perfect for this recipe.
- 1/3 cup low sodium soy sauce (lighter and healthier)
- 1/3 cup of rice wine vinegar for the sour part of recipe.
- 2 tablespoons of sugar for the sweet part.
- 3 tablespoons of Thai chili sauce (common in Asian cuisine and delicious.
- 1 teaspoon of ginger powder (an essential ingredient)
- 1 teaspoon of garlic

- 2 tablespoons of cornstarch to thicken the salmon sauce
- Chopped scallions for garnish, if desired.
- Sesame seeds for garnish on top of the salmon, if desired.

Instructions:

1. Preheat the oven to broil and position the oven rack to the top rack. Place the salmon fillets skin side down on a lined baking sheet sprayed with non-stick spray. Set aside.
2. In a small saucepan, combine soy sauce, rice wine vinegar, sugar, Thai chili sauce, ginger powder, garlic powder, and cornstarch. Bring to a simmer and whisk constantly until the sauce has thickened.
3. Brush half of the sauce on top the salmon fillets. Place in the oven and broil for about 7 to 10 minutes or until the salmon is fully cooked, brushing the salmon with the remaining sauce halfway through the cooking process. If the salmon starts to get too dark, then adjust the rack.
4. Once cooked, remove the skin and serve immediately with chopped scallions and sesame seeds for garnish, if desired.

Sweet and Sour Salmon can be served with:

➤ Brown Rice & Broccoli
➤ White Rice & Stir Fry Vegetables

- Lo Mein Noodles & Japanese Blend Vegetables
- Roasted Potatoes & Green Beans
- Mashed Cauliflower & Sauteed Asparagus

8

Thanksgiving is Every Meal

"Feed thankfulness, savor gratitude, and your plate of life will always be full."

As it says in Thessalonians 5:16-18: "Rejoice always, Pray continually, Give thanks in all circumstances; for this is God's will for you in Christ Jesus." Being thankful is about focusing on what's good in our lives and for the things that we have. It's about pausing to notice and appreciate the things that we often take for granted, like having a place to live, food to eat, clean water, friends, family, and a job to enable ourselves to pay bills. The key here is not just to be thankful once in a while but every day and for everything that we have… Appreciate All Things! Giving thanks is one of the highest honors that one can extend to another.

Giving thanks to yourself is perhaps even more powerful, for it is an acknowledgement that you have grown into the person you currently are. Even if you might not have enjoyed the process of getting to where you are, it is the journey of being "Thankful for all Things" that has shaped you into who you've become.

A Meal to be Thankful For Turkey Shepherd's Pie

Traditionally, shepherd's pie is made with chopped lamb, vegetables, and mashed potatoes. The meat is added to sautéed carrots, celery and onions, known in French cooking as a mirepoix. The gravy of the pie is made with meat stock, Worcestershire sauce, tomato paste and bay leaves. Shepherd's Pie can also be made with beef tips, ground beef, and there are vegetarian versions. For this recipe's instructions, it is prepared with ground turkey. In any case, with whatever version you select to prepare, it will be "A Meal to be Thankful For."

Ingredients:

- 1 pound Ground Turkey
- 1 medium Carrot, finely chopped
- 2 medium Celery rib, finely chopped
- 1 medium Onion, finely chopped
- 1 Bay leaf
- 1 ½ cup of Turkey stock
- 2 tablespoons of White Wine Sherry
- 1 tablespoon of Worcestershire sauce
- 1 tablespoon of Poultry Seasoning
- 4 tablespoons of unsalted Butter
- 3 tablespoons of All-Purpose Flour
- Salt and Pepper, to taste

Ingredients for Mashed Potatoes:

- 4 Large Potatoes, peeled and cut
- 2 tablespoons of Butter
- ¼ cup of Heavy Cream
- ¼ teaspoon Garlic powder

Instructions:

1. Preheat the oven to 350 degrees. Lightly coat a 2 ½ quart casserole dish with cooking spray or brush with oil.
2. Bring a medium saucepan with water to a boil, add a pinch of salt and potatoes. Reduce heat to a simmer and cook until the potatoes are fork tender, about 12 minutes.
3. Drain the potatoes thoroughly and return to the saucepan. Add heavy cream, butter and garlic powder, and mash until smooth. Cover and keep warm.
4. Meanwhile, heat butter in a large, heavy skillet over medium heat. Add carrots, celery, onions and then ground turkey, cook until ground turkey is done.
5. Reduce heat and add the white wine sherry, cook an additional minute, and add flour, mix thoroughly. Then add turkey stock, Worcestershire sauce, bay leaf, poultry seasoning, salt, and pepper to taste.
6. Cook until sauce is thickened, about 3 to 5 minutes.
7. Pour the turkey filling into the casserole dish. Spread the mashed potatoes over the turkey mixture. Sprinkle with paprika, if desired.
8. Transfer the casserole dish to the oven and bake for about 15 minutes or until the sauce is bubbling along the edges. Top with chopped chives if desired and serve.

Seven Sides to Serve with Shepherd's Pie:

- Garlic & Herb Dinner Rolls
- Baked Sweet Potato with Cinnamon Butter
- Maple Glazed Brussels Sprouts
- Butternut Squash & Apples Casserole
- Balsamic Roasted Green Beans
- Lemon Artichokes
- Sauteed Swiss Chard

9

The Journey of Seasons & Spices

There will be one thing in life that we can certainly count on: we will all, at some point or another, encounter challenging times. It's the nature of the life we live. The unavoidable "Ups and Downs" or, for the namesake of this chapter; **"Seasons & Spices,"** are sure to come our way. The daily hassles of life may tax our peace on a day-to-day basis. But when you've fallen on hard times and are experiencing a period of great difficulty, whether it's financially, personal, or health related, it can feel like a prison sentence. This may be tough, but you are tougher! Research has found that up to 70 percent of people experience positive psychology growth from difficult times. I believe that periods of hardships are there to teach us about endurance, perseverance, build our personal character, and strengthen our resilience. During those hard times, having strong coping strategies can make a huge difference. Of course, focusing on your spiritual life, exercising, eating healthier, and getting adequate rest are all good strategies. Being prepared for what's to come in all aspects of life is always the best strategy.

Drink Up

The 8th Wonder of the World Drink

Here is a drink for "The Ages." It has 8 "Incredible Ingredients" and will surely boost your spirit...Anywhere & Anytime!!

That's why I call it "The 8th Wonder of the World Drink."

Ingredients:

- 20 ounces Carrot Juice
- 1 tablespoon of Ginger Powder
- 1 tablespoon of Beet Powder
- 1 tablespoon of Moringa Powder
- 1 tablespoon of Turmeric Powder
- 1 tablespoon of Black Plum Powder
- 1 tablespoon of Green Tea Powder
- 1 tablespoon of Ground Cinnamon

Yields: Two 10oz. Servings

Instructions:

Pour carrot juice into the blender and add all remaining ingredients, blend until incorporated. Drink, be happy and healthy!!!

10

The Melting Pot

Having had the opportunity to travel at a young age and later to travel more while serving in the military, I came to realize that some of the people in this world are amazing. I've been fascinated by other people and their backgrounds during the course of my travels. I'm passionately intrigued by the differences in each of us because it helps us to understand each other better. We learn from each other and become stronger when we embrace our differences. Even though we all are in **"The Melting Pot"** of life together, we remain different, and diversity in any dimension can be used to differentiate groups and people from one another. In a nutshell, it's about empowering people by respecting and appreciating what makes them different, in terms of age, gender, ethnicity, religion, disability, sexual orientation, education, and national origin. Overall, being together in the melting pot of diversity is important because it can lead to better outcomes in various aspects of life, fostering creativity, innovation, empathy, and social cohesion. It also helps create a more just and inclusive society where everyone has an opportunity to succeed. And my perspective as it relates to the diverse unification of **Us All** is; If I don't succeed and you don't succeed, then **We All** do not succeed...

Diversity Stew

Harty Vegetable Vegan Stew

You'll find a number of plant-based stew recipes out there with a host of ingredients ranging from fresh garden vegetables, soy protein, mushrooms, grains, rice, potatoes, beans, and lentils. With all of the ingredients that are available, it makes it hard to choose a favorite. They are all equally delicious stews but also uniquely different in the way they deliver their deliciousness. This Vegan Stew recipe is:

Ingredients:

- 2 Plant-Based Patties, seared and cut into ¼-inch cubes (brand of choice)
- 2 Large Potatoes, peeled and cut into ½-inch cubes
- 4 medium Mushrooms, sliced
- 2 Large Carrots, peeled and cut into ¼-inch rounds
- 2 Celery ribs, medium diced
- 1 Onion, medium diced
- 2 Garlic Cloves, minced
- ½ cup of frozen Green Peas, thawed
- 5 cups of Vegetable Broth, homemade or low-sodium can
- 1 cup of Red Wine
- 2 small Bay Leaves
- 1 tablespoon of Thyme
- 2 tablespoons of Olive Oil
- ¼ cup of Roux, cooked equal parts butter & flour
- Salt & fresh ground Pepper, to taste

Yield: 4 servings

Instructions:

1. In a large stock pot, heat olive oil, then add carrots, onions, and celery, sauté for about 3 minutes.
2. Add cubed potatoes, mushrooms, garlic, and red wine into the pot, cook for an addition 3 minutes.
3. Pour in the vegetable broth and add the plant-based cubes, peas, bay leaves, and thyme. Salt and pepper to taste.
4. Reduce heat and simmer for 20 minutes or until potatoes and carrots are tender. Whisk in roux a little at a time until desired thickness.
5. Remove from heat and serve.

   *Here are some other vegan/vegetarian stew variations:

- ➤ Vegan Black Bean Stew
- ➤ Curried Vegetable Stew
- ➤ Vegan Lentil Stew
- ➤ Creamy Vegan Mushroom Stew
- ➤ Vegan Irish Stew
- ➤ Sweet Potato & Peanut Butter Stew
- ➤ Vegan Eggplant Stew
- ➤ Mexican Quinoa Vegan Stew

11

Time to Serve

I talked about the importance of managing your time in chapter three. Time carries a whole lot of weight in your life's process; it is associated with everything that you do. The evolutionary process of human survival is to give back, pass on, if you will, all that we've learned and experienced in our past time to the next generation and so on. It's our God-given duty; it is our **"Time to Serve"**. Your time is precious, and gifting it back can make a world of difference in the lives of many. Finding time to do anything, let alone make time for someone else, can be difficult. The other thing about time is that it's a limited resource; you can't go back and get more when you run out. This means that giving the "service of your time" may be one of the most valuable gifts you can give to someone! To give back, you have to give up something, whether time, resources or experience. Giving back or serving entails sacrifice. You have to sacrifice time, money, knowledge, and resources that you could have used for yourself. When you're in a position to have gotten so much, the gift at this point is giving back the service of your time. Remember what we do in life is stitched in the record of time.

Cooking Times of Service

The precise origins of cooking are unknown, but at some point in the distant past, early humans conquered fire and started using it to prepare food. Presently there are three types of cooking methods:

- Dry Heat Cooking
- Moist Heat Cooking
- Combination Cooking (involves both dry and moist heat cooking).

And each method is how we use heat to cook food and bring out the unique flavors and textures in what we are cooking. Food preparation is about timing, and timing is important in cooking. Here are some common cooking techniques that can be a factor in your preparation time of service:

Baking: Is a method of preparing food that uses dry heat, typically in an oven, but can also be done on hot ashes or on hot stone. The most common baked item is bread, but many other types of food can be baked.

Frying: Is a cooking technique in which food is cooked in hot oil or fats. Pan-frying is when food is cooked in a frying pan with oil. Deep-frying is when food is completely immersed in hot oil. Stir-frying is when you fry food very quickly on high heat in an oiled stir-fry pan or wok.

Grilling: Is a dry-heat cooking technique. Food is cooked on metal grates that are placed over a heat source in order to produce a smokey, charred flavor. Grills can use gas, electricity, charcoal or wood. Meats, poultry, fish and vegetables can all be grilled.

Roasting: Is a cooking technique that uses dry heat where hot air covers the food, cooking it evenly on all sides with temperatures of at least 300 degrees from an open flame, oven, or other heat source. Roasting can enhance the flavor through caramelization browning on the surface of the food.

Boiling: Is a moist heat technique that cooks food in boiling water or other water-based liquids (stock, broth, milk, etc.). The temperature for boiling is 212 degrees or when the liquid that you are using for cooking has rapid bubbles.

Simmering: Is a cooking technique that brings the liquid of a dish to just below the boiling point over lower heat. This method uses moderate heat to soften foods slowly over time, before gradually adding seasoning and other ingredients to the food being cooked.

Stewing: Is a slow cooking method, similar to braising, with the difference being that the food being cooked is covered in liquid. Stewing is best done in a heavy stock pot, on the stovetop, or in a slow-cooker.

Sauteing: Is a cooking technique which derives its name from the French verb for jumping. Sautee' is a dry-heat cooking method, which involves cooking a small amount of fat in a hot pan, then tossing the ingredients around.

Braising: Is a combination cooking technique that uses both dry and moist heats. Typically, the food is first browned at a high temperature, then simmered in a covered pot in a cooking liquid (wine, broth or stock). It is similar to stewing but uses less liquid.

Steaming: Is a technique of cooking that requires moist heat. The heat is created by boiling water which vaporizes into steam. The steam brings heat to the food and cooks it. Unlike boiling, the food is separate from the water and only comes into direct contact with the steam.

Microwaving: Is a cooking method that quickly cooks, heats, and thaws food for the shortest amount of time, and uses as little liquid as possible.

Air Frying: Uses convection heat to cook foods so that they are browned and crispy on the outside but remain moist and tender on the inside. Cooking with an air fryer takes less time and makes less of a mess than deep frying or traditional oven roasting.

It's Time to Cook Something…

12

Beyond the Two Layer Cake

When I think of layers in regards to cooking, I also think of levels. In the context of this chapter, I envision human potential as the ability to taking something desired, to accomplish and succeed, to another level, the next level, or the highest level. To do and be better than average! The **Level of Layers** in which to maximize our human potential is vast and without limits; it is steps with endless stairs, it is ocean waves that don't stop, it is a ladder that reaches beyond the stratosphere. The limits you perceive are nothing but your own thinking inside a box. The question of how you can think bigger is not only in your thoughts but in your attitude. How you think is important. And it is you who can excel in any aspect of your life by reaching beyond your limited beliefs. Two of my quotes to share regarding this statement are: "Move from Limitless Beliefs to Believing that there are no Limitations" and the other one is: "Reach up Beyond the Stratosphere to Grab Your Destiny." Pushing beyond your limits helps to improve your self-worth. It will help you understand that you can get through tough situations if need be. It will also give you the ability and strength to build the layers needed towards reaching your goals.

Your Cake Layers

Gemini Brownie Marble Cake

If you noticed throughout the previous chapters, I emphasized and made points of things in twos. Being born on the twin sign, maybe that's the Gemini in me. Regardless, you're going to like building this two-tier Gemini Cake recipe.

Ingredients for Brownie Mix:

- 1 cup of All-Purpose Flour
- 1 cup of unsweetened Cocoa
- 1 cup of granulated Sugar
- ½ cup of melted Butter
- 2 Eggs
- 1 teaspoon of Vanilla Extract
- 1 tablespoon of Water
- ½ teaspoon of Salt

Instructions:

In a mixing bowl, whisk together all the ingredients until well blended. Spread brownie mixture in a 9" round cake pan that has been sprayed with cooking spray. Bake at 350 degrees for about 20-25 minutes. Cool, remove from pan, and place it on a cake stand or plate for the base of the marble cake.

Ingredients for Marble Cake:

- 2 ¾ cups of Cake Flour
- 2 teaspoons of Baking Powder
- ½ teaspoon of salt
- 1 cup of unsalted Butter, room temperature
- 2 cups of granulated Sugar
- 4 large Eggs
- 1 ¼ cup of Buttermilk
- 1 tablespoon of Vanilla Extract
- 4 oz. of Dark or semi-sweet Chocolate, chopped

Instructions:

1. Preheat oven to 350 degrees. Butter and flour 2 (9-inch) cake pans and wrap the pans with cake strips if desired.
2. In a large bowl, whisk together flour, baking powder, and salt.
3. In a mixer stand mixing bowl, fitted with a paddle attachment, beat butter on medium speed until creamy. Add the sugar and beat until light and fluffy. Add eggs and beat until well combined.

4. With the mixer on low, slowly add the buttermilk, vanilla extract, and flour mixture to create the cake batter. Using a rubber spatula, divide the batter among the 2 prepared cake pans.
5. Melt the chocolate in the microwave in 20-second intervals, stirring until smooth. Spoon the melted chocolate over the plain cake batter, dividing between the 2 pans. Using the tip of a knife, swirl the chocolate and cake batter together slightly.
6. Bake both cakes for 30 to 35 minutes or until completely firm in the middle. Let the cakes cool until ready to assemble.

Ingredients for Chocolate Buttercream Frosting:

- 1½ cups of unsalted Butter, room temperature
- 1/3 cup unsweetened Cocoa Powder
- 5 ¾ cups of Confectioners' Sugar
- 1 teaspoon of Vanilla Extract
- 5 tablespoons of Heavy Whipping Cream
- Chocolate & White Chocolate squeeze bottle syrup (any brand)

Instructions:

1. In the bowl of a stand mixer fitted with the paddle attachment, beat the butter on medium speed for about 2 minutes until it becomes creamy.
2. Add cocoa powder to the bowl and mix on low just until combined. Scrape the bowl down.
3. With the mixer on low speed, beat in the confectioners' sugar a little at a time. Then beat in the heavy whipping cream and vanilla. Turn the speed up to medium and beat until the frosting is well blended and fluffy.

Assembling Instructions:

1. Trim the tops of the cakes to create even layers if needed.
2. Spread a thin layer of frosting on top of the brownie that was placed on the cake stand or plate earlier. Place one cake layer on top of the frosted brownie.
3. Spread about ½ cup of the frosting over the top, place the last cake on top and spread the remaining frosting all over the top and sides of the entire cake and brownie layers.
4. Spread frosting in a smooth style. With both chocolate/white chocolate syrups, squeeze round (circle)

designs on top of cake. Chill cake for at least 1 hour or until ready to serve.

Don't let the Recipe of your Life's

Potential die with you...

About the Author

Chef Marvin Jones, Founder and CEO of ChefM Services, is a culinary artist served in the United States Marine Corps for eight years as a Food Service Specialist and graduated from The Restaurant School of Philadelphia at Walnut Hill College, with specialized training in Culinary Arts and Business Management.

In 2010, he established ChefM Services, a company that provides comprehensive services in all areas of food preparation and cooking for all occasions. Chef Marvin is a highly sought-after Chef, Entrepreneur, Author, Motivational Writer, Positive Change Agent, and Philanthropist.

His Entrepreneur Endeavors Encompass:

- **Philosophy of Vegan & Gourmet Healthy Cooking**

- **Author of a Three Book Trilogy:**

1. Recipes of Motivation
2. Live Your Life Larger than the Portions on Your Plate
3. On the Cutting Edge

Additional Ventures Include:

- Creative Cooking with ChefM – An innovative Cooking Show
- From the Creative Hands of ChefM – Cook Books
- Starvin Like Marvin Publications
- Freight Train Jones Productions
- On the Cutting Edge/Video Marketing
- Fitness Chef Services/Fitness Training & Meal Preparation

Contact Details:

Phone: ChefM Services - 1-888-243-3617

Email: ChefMServices@gmail.com

ChefMServices.com

Made in the USA
Middletown, DE
19 June 2024